THE
CHEROKEE

by Barbara A. McCall

Illustrated by Luciano Lazzarino

ROURKE PUBLICATIONS, INC.

VERO BEACH, FLORIDA 32964

CONTENTS

Library of Congress Cataloging-in-Publication Data

McCall, Barbara A., 1936–
  The Cherokee / by Barbara A. McCall.
    p. cm. —(Native American people)
  Summary: Examines the history, traditional lifestyle, and current situation of the Cherokee Indians.
    1. Cherokee Indians—Juvenile literature. [1. Cherokee Indians. 2. Indians of North America.] I. Title. II. Series.
  E99.C5M38 1989   973'.0497—dc19
      ISBN 0-86625-376-9   88-3947

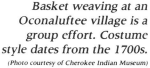

INTRODUCTION

Thousands of years ago, during the last Ice Age, groups of people began to migrate from Asia to the Americas. They probably crossed a land bridge that stretched between the lands that are now Siberia and Alaska. Slowly the groups moved south and east in search of lands where the hunting was good.

When Columbus reached America, he found the descendants of these peoples and called them Indians. Today we recognize the Indians as the only true native Americans.

They are members of the ethnic race of people called Mongols, which also includes peoples of China and Japan. They have straight black hair, and high cheekbones.

The way of life of the Native Americans was quite different from that of the white settlers who moved into their territory. Indians believed that the land belonged to a whole tribe. No part belonged to the individual. This was contrary to the beliefs of the Europeans, who were eager to possess their own parcels of land in the New World.

When whites first came among the Cherokees, the Indians held ancestral lands that extended from Virginia to Florida and west across the Appalachian Mountains almost to the Mississippi River. Quickly those lands were lost to the New Americans—the European settlers and their descendants.

Indians have often been pictured as wild, savage, warlike peoples. That is an untrue picture. The Cherokees, in particular, were an intelligent, hardworking, and peace-loving tribe.

The Cherokee and four other southern tribes were known as the Five Civilized Tribes. All were eventually forced to leave their eastern homelands and migrate to the area that one day would become the state of Oklahoma.

The U.S. government treated the Cherokees with dishonor and dishonesty for nearly 150 years. It was not until 1924 that all Indians were recognized as citizens of the United States. Since then, Native Americans have gradually gained some of the respect and rights to which they are entitled.

the
Cherokee

Reservation in
Indian Territory

Trail of Tears

Original Cherokee
Homeland

Cherokee Eagle Dance enacted outside the Cherokee Museum.

Before the White Men

WHAT was life like among the Indians before the whites arrived? No one knows exactly, but historians are certain that the Indians of the Southeast had a highly advanced civilization. Thanks to archeologists, we have a partial picture of those early years. Archeologists hunt for remains of early civilizations and study those remains, called artifacts. Archeologists dig up the earth looking for artifacts that will help them piece together the mysterious puzzle of the early years.

One of the best known Indian artifacts is the arrowhead. This piece of stone was not part of an arrow at all. It was a point for a dart or spear. Nevertheless, archeologists used these pieces as time markers to tell when Indians lived in a certain place. The shape of the arrowhead changed over time, and scientists have excavated some that go back thousands of years.

Let us travel back in time about five hundred years and look at a Cherokee town. In the center of the town was a large square or plaza. Around the center were several large mounds. The homes of the Indians were clustered around these mounds. Sometimes the mounds served as platforms for large houses for the chief and other important members of the tribe. Most Indians lived in smaller houses on the ground.

These houses were built of lightweight materials. Tree bark, reeds, and grasses were used. Mud houses were also built. These were made from upright poles, with reeds woven between the poles. The mud was then layered over the poles and reeds. The roof was made of thatch or overlapped bark. Each town also had a large round council house that served as a ceremonial hall. It could seat 400 to 500 people.

The Cherokees were expert farmers. They raised corn, beans, squash, pumpkins, sunflowers, and tobacco. Their farm fields circled their towns, and the women tended the farms. Each family had its own farm plot. Every town also had a communal field to provide food for the poor and travelers. The women also gathered wild plant food, such as berries and nuts. It was the job of the men to hunt, fish, and chop down trees to make dugout canoes.

Hunting was the men's main occupation. They used bows and arrows, blowguns, spears, snares, and other kinds of traps. Deer was the most important game animal because it was used for both food and clothing. The Indians made most of their clothing from skins of various animals or from woven fibers of the hemp plant. The women wore wrap-around and knee-length skirts. Both men and women wore deerskin moccasins that reached halfway to the knee. Men wore a breechclout—a piece of fabric about 18 inches wide that passed between the legs and was held at the waist by a belt. The ends hung down in front and back almost to the knees.

At first, Indians only killed animals they needed for food and clothing. The arrival of the whites changed that. It was then that the Indians began to slaughter great numbers of animals to obtain skins and furs to trade with the settlers.

The Cherokee Indians had lived in one place for many years. This was unusual among the northern Indians. Because the Cherokees were great farmers who lived in permanent towns, the white traders and settlers quickly thought of them as being civilized.

But the Cherokees were warriors, too. They often needed to defend themselves from raids by the Iroquois from the north and attacks by the Chickasaw, who lived along the Mississippi River. Sometimes the Cherokees would take the offensive and raid other tribes in search of new hunting grounds, wives, and slaves.

Before a war party left a town, many ceremonial rituals took place. There was fasting, dancing, body painting, and smoking. Smoking was tied to many ceremonies. Archeologists have uncovered great numbers of pipes in many varieties. Some were made of pottery; others were made of stone. Many were designed with figures that represented animals. Human figures adorned others.

In every Cherokee village there was a male war chief and a peace chief. The peace chief was always a female. Her advice was listened to by men and women alike. The Cherokee female was also head of the family. All children were members of the mother's family. If the father was killed, his wife and children were cared for by the wife's brother. If a Cherokee woman married a white trader or settler, her children considered themselves primarily Cherokee, even after many generations of white fathers.

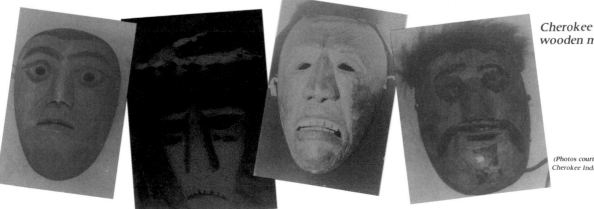

Cherokee wooden masks.

(Photos courtesy of Cherokee Indian Museum)

Early Traders and Explorers

In 1540, the Cherokees met their first white man—Hernando DeSoto. He was a Spanish explorer who traveled with his soldiers from Florida to the beautiful green Appalachian Mountains of what is now northern Georgia and western North Carolina. They were in search of gold. DeSoto never found gold, but this meeting of Indian and European was important. It was the beginning of a long history of Cherokee contact with white men and women who would change the future for all Native Americans.

The Spanish often treated the Cherokees cruelly and owned them like slaves. But the Spanish introduced the Indians to new and wonderful things—knives of steel that did not break as easily as Indian knives did. The stone axes used by the Indians were not sharp, and it often took days to fell a tree. The Spanish brought axes of iron that could cut trees in hours.

The Cherokee women were amazed by the soft garments of brightly colored cloth that DeSoto's soldiers wore beneath their armor. The women discovered how to sew with steel needles rather than needles made from animal bone.

About one hundred years later, French explorers traveled south from Canada and made contact with the Cherokees. The French were primarily friendly traders. They wanted skins and furs that the Cherokee men trapped so skillfully. The various Indian tribes often warred among themselves to gain the best hunting grounds. The fur trade caused much bloodshed among Indian neighbors competing for control of the richest land. The Indians exchanged deerskins plus furs of wolf, beaver, and fox for the wonders of the white men—steel knives and axes, needles, scissors, copper pots, glass beads, mirrors, woolen blankets, and colored cloth.

In addition to supplying these fine products of the European civilization, the French were probably the first to provide the Cherokees with guns. In part, the guns were to make hunting easier and more rewarding. But the French also wanted the support of the Cherokees against the British traders and colonists who were moving over the mountains from their towns and cities along the Atlantic coast.

The Creek Indians and Nancy Ward

From time to time the Cherokees battled with the neighboring tribes. But the Creeks were their most persistent enemies. Conflicts between the two tribes dragged on for nearly thirty years until 1755. Then the most decisive and hard fought battle between the two tribes occurred at Tali'wa in Georgia. The Cherokees were outnumbered two to one by the Creeks. A retreat was planned, until a heroic young Cherokee woman rallied the Cherokee warriors.

That woman was 16-year-old Nancy Ward. She was alongside her husband, loading his rifles, when he was killed. Nancy then took up his gun and fought with such courage that the Cherokee men were inspired to fight again with great vigor. The warriors regrouped and pressed on to victory. After that battle, the Creeks abandoned their interest in Cherokee lands. The two lived in peace side by side until the battle of Horseshoe Bend more than 60 years later.

Nancy Ward is probably the best known Cherokee woman. When the American Revolution raged, Nancy sometimes warned white settlers of coming attacks. She also interceded for their safety when they were taken captive. Perhaps the most remarkable activity of this woman occurred when she served as the principal spokesperson in a treaty negotiation.

Wars with the Settlers

Between 1754 and 1763, the British and French were at war in North America to determine who would control different parts of the New World. Many Indians fought for the French, and so these battles were called the French and Indian Wars. But the Cherokee warriors joined the British forces during most of these battles.

A Cherokee leader by the name of Ostenaco was a trusted aid to three British colonial governors. With a band of warriors, he also assisted Colonel George Washington and the Virginia militia who were struggling against the overwhelming strength of the French troops.

Washington said of these Cherokees: "They are more serviceable than twice their number of white men . . . upon these people the safety of our march very much depends." In 1762 Ostenaco traveled to London, where he was received in full honor by King George III.

The British defeated the French and in doing so gained control of America between the Atlantic Ocean and the Mississippi River and north to Canada. The Cherokees were on the winning side and had gained the friendship of the British— at least for a while.

The American Revolution

Despite problems with some colonists, the Cherokees generally got along well with their white neighbors before the American Revolution. Between the years 1765 and 1775, the Cherokees and whites lived mainly in peace. White traders married into Indian families. Family names like Ross, Lowrey, Taylor, and Smith began to appear within the tribe. The children of these marriages slowly adopted the ways of the white parent, but they remembered that a child of a Cherokee mother was first and always a Cherokee.

The old-style Cherokee mud house was replaced by a log cabin, much like those built by whites fearless enough to make their homes in the wilderness. Cherokee women began to model their clothes after white women, using the soft cloth traded for Indian skins.

With the coming of the Revolutionary War, peaceful coexistence with the white man had collapsed. The Cherokees supported the British and King George III. The Indian warriors took to the warpath against settlers from Virginia to Georgia. In small towns, men were killed, and the women and children were taken to Cherokee towns as prisoners. The Cherokees earned the reputation of being savage devils. But the same reputation could have been applied to the whites who quickly retaliated against their Indian attackers. Cherokee villages were burned and women and children were sold into slavery in the West Indies.

The Cherokee suffered greatly for sid-

ing with the British against the rebelling colonists. When the Revolution ended in 1781, the Indians paid a heavy penalty for being on the losing side. The fighting between the Cherokees and the new Americans continued. Those settlers who had been living in Cherokee territory wanted more land and more revenge. And they got both. Many Cherokees were brutally driven from their homes. Some were forced to find shelter in the woods or mountains.

After several years of abuse, the Indians decided they could no longer try to hold out against the invading white settlers. In order to end the conflict, the Indians agreed to cede many of their lands to the new American nation. Thirty-nine Cherokee leaders signed the Treaty of Tellico in 1789 and the Treaty of Holston in 1791. The treaties ceded to the United States most of the Cherokee homeland in what is now North Carolina, South Carolina, and Tennessee. The Indians still would control about 43,000 square miles in Georgia and Alabama, as well as lands in the Great Smoky Mountains of the Appalachians.

These treaties, signed by George Washington, stated that the Cherokees could live on their remaining lands "as long as the rivers flowed and the grass grew." Of course, the greed of the white men forced the United States to dishonor these treaties.

Between this time and 1902, the Cherokees signed 25 treaties with the white men. No other tribe signed more treaties than the Cherokee. Eighteen of those treaties gave away tribal lands of what was once the largest Indian territory in the South.

11

A Great Nation Grows

As the size of the Cherokee lands diminished, the talents and accomplishments of the Cherokee people expanded. Or so it seemed. By 1800 the Cherokees once again lived harmoniously with white pioneers around them.

The Cherokee sons of white traders and settlers became prosperous landowners and adopted the lifestyle of the white people. Some Indians owned large plantations, raising cotton and trading successfully with Northerners.

Most Cherokee men were good farmers who became even more skillful and productive with iron plows purchased from whites. Cherokee women excelled at weaving fine cloth. Now they used European spinning wheels and looms. Most Indians dressed like whites. However, some men chose to wear a tunic and turban—a compromise between white and Indian ways.

As time passed the Cherokees built small towns, complete with roads, stores, schools, and churches. They invited white Christian missionaries to teach their young people to read and write English. Most Indians were not interested in becoming Christian, although many did. But the Cherokee leaders knew the missionaries would help their people adapt more quickly to the fast-moving world of the white men.

The Cherokee people were determined to be a part of the white man's world, yet distinct from it. By 1796, the Cherokees began to develop their own form of central government, modeled in a fashion after the U.S. government. The Indians abandoned their old system of many villages, each with its own chief. The new central system provided for a democratic form of government. There would be one principal chief who would preside over all Cherokees, wherever they lived. Each village or town had a representative on the council that made laws for all members of the Cherokee tribe. This move made the Indians more united and more powerful. It was the birth of the Cherokee Nation, a title that would be used from that time forward.

But other Indian tribes had hopes of shaping the Indian world into a powerful force against the whites. Tecumseh, leader and famous warrior of the Shawnee Indians, dreamed of an alliance of all Indian tribes of the East. He saw a strong union as a means for all Indians to protect their lands from the advances of whites who were usurping the territories of all Indians much too quickly.

Tecumseh traveled from his home in the Ohio Valley to seek support from the powerful Creek Indians and the new Cherokee Nation. He was successful in gaining agreement from the Creeks for his idea of an Indian alliance. But the Cherokees rejected Tecumseh's plan. The Cherokee leaders knew that in war, the Indians' knives, tomahawks, and guns would be a poor match against the whites who had cannons and endless supplies of gunpowder.

Tecumseh, the leader of the Shawnee Indians.

The Creeks and Shawnees were soon at war with the U.S. Army, under the leadership of General Andrew Jackson. About 800 Cherokees gave their support to Jackson and rode with the soldiers against other Indians. In 1813 at the battle of Horseshoe Bend, along the Tallipoosa River in Alabama, things seemed hopeless for Jackson's troops. The Creeks were too strong for the Army. But the Cherokee saved the battle by swimming across the river and attacking the Creeks from the rear. Following the battle, the Cherokee celebrated the victory with a ceremonial eagle dance. (The eagle is a highly honored animal among the Cherokees.) Tecumseh was killed, and with

The Cherokee admired the eagle.

him died the Indian dream of halting the westward push of the pioneers. There would be no more grand attempts to lock the whites into lands along the Eastern shores.

The Cherokees had proven their loyalty to the U.S. government and Andrew Jackson by fighting in the war against the Creeks, but the government and Jackson were soon to demonstrate that they had no loyalty to the Cherokee Indians.

Andrew Jackson would one day become President of the United States and completely ignore the loyal support of these Indians. But during the years before Jackson's presidency, the Cherokee Nation would continue to grow.

Sequoyah developed the first written Indian language.

(Photo courtesy of Cherokee Indian Museum)

Sequoyah and the Syllabary

The greatest accomplishment of the Cherokee Nation was the invention of a written language. The person responsible for this remarkable feat was a man named Sequoyah. He was born in the village of Tuskegee on the Tennessee River about ten years before the Revolutionary War. Sequoyah was the son of an Indian woman and a white trader. His English name was George Guess.

Although Sequoyah had no official schooling, he was very bright, creative, and ambitious. He taught himself to be a silversmith, which no other Cherokee had been. He became a skilled blacksmith, too. And he sketched and painted pictures of horses and other animals.

But one skill attracted Sequoyah more than any other. That was the ability of the powerful whites to read and write. That ability, Sequoyah believed, was the source of the whites' power. The whites could store their knowledge in books that could be passed from generation to generation. They could communicate across the oceans by means of "talking leaves"—the name Sequoyah gave to the pages of letters and books. The Indians, on the other hand, could convey information only through direct communication from person to person.

If the Cherokee had a written language, Sequoyah believed, they would be better able to protect their lands. So, in the year 1809, Sequoyah began the long process of creating a written language. At first he attempted to design a symbol for

16

each word in the Cherokee language. But such a system was too cumbersome. He abandoned that approach, but he did not give up his dream.

Sequoyah moved from whole words to sounds within words—syllables. After years of listening very carefully to all the sounds in the words of his native language, Sequoyah was able to identify 85 sounds or syllables. He then gave each syllable a symbol. Some symbols were modeled after the English alphabet and some conceived totally from his creative imagination.

After working on his language for more than ten years, Sequoyah had succeeded in creating not an alphabet but a syllabary. This was the first written Indian language. But his task was not completed until he could convince others to learn and use his invention.

The first person to learn the new syllabary was Sequoyah's young son. Sequoyah wanted to demonstrate to the chiefs of his tribe that even a child could learn to use the new language. In 1821 he had the opportunity he was looking for. Many leading tribesmen gathered to watch him make mysterious markings on paper while they talked. He wrote down a few words spoken by one chief and had a messenger take the written words to his son who was standing at a distance. Sequoyah's son of course, could read the words.

All who had gathered were amazed. But most thought Sequoyah had performed some kind of magic or sorcery. They were not convinced of the value of the strange symbols. But one leader was intrigued enough to want to know more about the syllabary. This was just what Sequoyah had hoped would happen. He then arranged to teach the syllabary to a group of men. Very quickly the men were able to write messages dictated to them by the elders. Finally everyone was convinced that Sequoyah had created a truly remarkable feat.

Sequoyah was considered a hero by his people and by others. And justly so! He was the only person in history to create an entire written language. And he made it possible for the Cherokees to claim the honor of having the first written Indian language.

The many years that Sequoyah devoted to crafting a written language were anything but calm, quiet days. During those years, he rode with other Cherokee warriors to fight alongside Andrew Jackson and the U.S. Army in the War of 1812 and the Creek War.

After that, Sequoyah and others from his village gave up their efforts to resist the invasions of land-greedy settlers. The whole village migrated from their home along the Tennessee River to a new village along the Arkansas River.

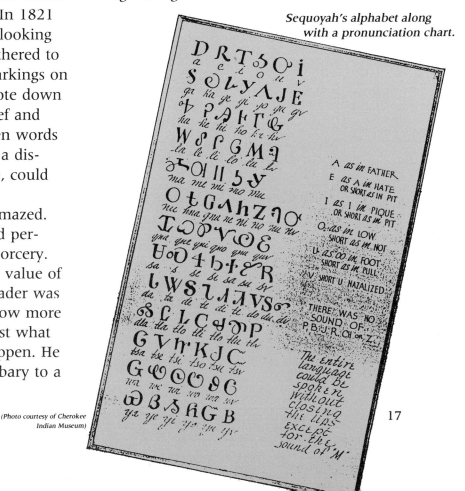

Sequoyah's alphabet along with a pronunciation chart.

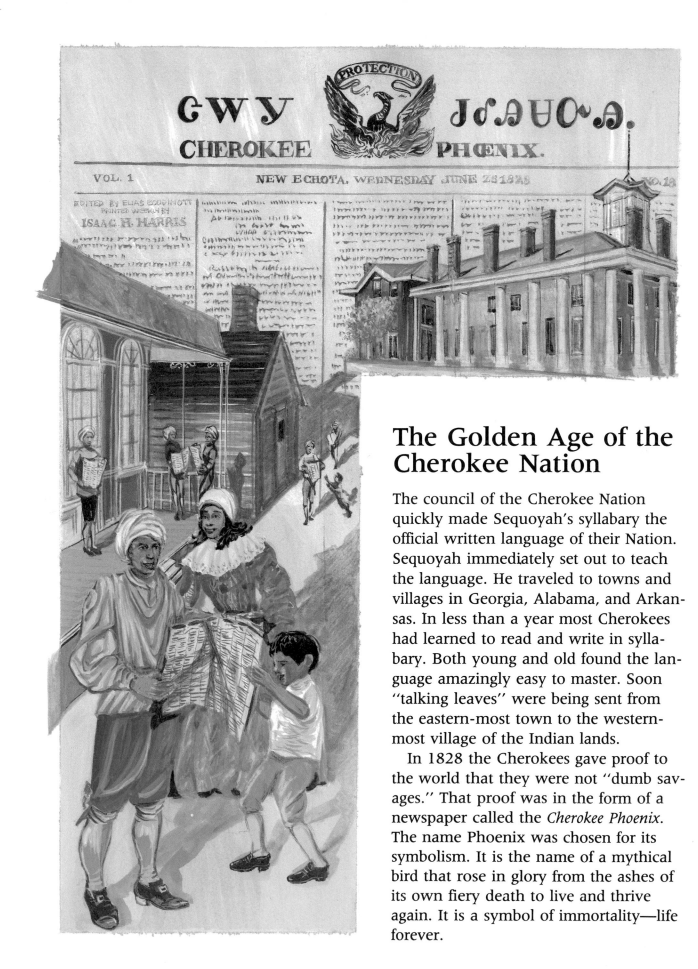

The Golden Age of the Cherokee Nation

The council of the Cherokee Nation quickly made Sequoyah's syllabary the official written language of their Nation. Sequoyah immediately set out to teach the language. He traveled to towns and villages in Georgia, Alabama, and Arkansas. In less than a year most Cherokees had learned to read and write in syllabary. Both young and old found the language amazingly easy to master. Soon "talking leaves" were being sent from the eastern-most town to the western-most village of the Indian lands.

In 1828 the Cherokees gave proof to the world that they were not "dumb savages." That proof was in the form of a newspaper called the *Cherokee Phoenix*. The name Phoenix was chosen for its symbolism. It is the name of a mythical bird that rose in glory from the ashes of its own fiery death to live and thrive again. It is a symbol of immortality—life forever.

The paper was printed in Cherokee and English. It was distributed nationally to both Indians and whites. The paper was even read in England. That should not be surprising, since the Cherokees and British had been strong allies before the Revolutionary War.

The leaders of the Cherokee Nation foolishly hoped that their progress as a civilized nation would make them more acceptable to whites. But the leaders hoped in vain. Neither the illiterate frontiersman nor the President of the United States was willing to honor the rights of the Indians. These Native Americans controlled valuable territory that the new Americans were determined to have for themselves.

The Cherokee Nation established its capital in the town of New Echota, Georgia. In 1828 the great John Ross was elected Principal Chief. Ross was a brilliant man who would guide the Cherokees through their most troublesome and painful years. Ross was the son of a Scottish immigrant and a Cherokee mother. He was only one-eighth Chero-

Printing press for Cherokee Phoenix.

kee. When Ross married, he chose a full-blooded Cherokee wife, Quatie, and devoted his whole life to his people.

When Chief Ross took office, he governed more than 17,000 Indians—about 15,000 living in Georgia and Alabama, with the rest in the new territory of Arkansas. Ross spoke the Cherokee language with some difficulty. He preferred English. When he addressed the council, he needed an interpreter.

During the late 1820s and early 1830s, the Cherokee Nation developed into a highly cultured and organized civilization. That time was called the golden age—their finest hour. The Cherokee were a literate and democratic people. They had a constitution, written first in English in 1817 and rewritten in Cherokee on July 27, 1827. They had their own postal system, their own police force, and a two-house legislature. The Cherokee had great promise for further development, but it was not to happen. They would soon be driven brutally from their homelands, never to regain their former status.

(Photo courtesy of Cherokee Indian Museum)

Chief John Ross.

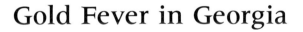

Gold Fever in Georgia

In 1828 gold was discovered at Dahlonega, Georgia, in the heart of Cherokee land. White miners, greedy for quick wealth, invaded the area. They stole Indian cattle, attacked Indian women, and drove families from their homes.

Young Cherokee men wanted to retaliate against the gangs of whites who terrorized, plundered, and burned their homes. But the elders of the tribe persuaded the young against more violence, believing that violence would only make matters worse. Instead the Cherokees would seek justice from the courts. But there was no justice from Georgia courts.

Finally Chief John Ross appealed to President Andrew Jackson for help. Ross asked for army troops to stop the vio-

lence. A few troops were sent, but they could not control the miners. Or, perhaps, they did not want to anger their fellow whites. Ross took further steps to obtain justice for his people. He hired a Philadelphia lawyer to take the Cherokee case before the U.S. Supreme Court.

Chief Justice John Marshall ruled in 1832 that the federal government must protect the Cherokee people from white law breakers. But President Jackson had no intention to act upon Justice Marshall's ruling. Jackson said, "John Marshall has rendered his decision; let him enforce it, if he can."

While the Cherokee were seeking help from Washington, the state of Georgia was illegally passing laws against the Cherokee people who were part of the independent Cherokee Nation. Georgia declared that the Cherokee Nation was only a county of Georgia. It was therefore subject to Georgia laws. One of these new laws stated that Indians could not mine gold even on their own land. Another law stated that a Cherokee could not testify against a white person in court.

Georgia was determined to end the power and independence of Cherokees. Martial law was imposed on the Cherokee Nation. The *Cherokee Phoenix* was forced to shut down. And Chief Ross was imprisoned. Other Indians were arrested and jailed on the slightest excuse. Whites who committed crimes against the Indians were not punished. In every way possible, the Cherokees were persecuted by Georgians in an effort to force the Indians out of the state.

21

The Indian Removal Act

While the Cherokee Nation was fighting for survival in Georgia and pleading for justice in Washington, the U.S. government passed the Indian Removal Act of 1830. President Andrew Jackson successfully persuaded Congress to pass this law that affected all Indians in the Southeast. The Act called for the removal, by force if necessary, of all Indians living east of the Mississippi. The Indians were to be resettled on land west of the river, in a place called the Indian Territory. One day that land would become known as Oklahoma.

For decades, the federal government talked about some way to move the Indians off their lands. A few Indians had voluntarily moved during those years, rather than to fight a losing battle. But the Cherokee Nation and other southern tribes were stubborn peoples. They did not want to move from the land that was rightfully theirs. Five tribes in all were affected by the Act. In addition to the Cherokees, there were the Creek, Chickasaw, Choctaw, and Seminole tribes. These tribes were called the Five Civilized Tribes.

The Georgia state legislature wasted no time in preparing for the enforcement of the Removal Act. In 1832 the state passed the Cherokee Land Lottery. This allowed the state to sell all the Indian lands in North Georgia, even before the Indians left the lands. Lottery winners were given 160-acre farms or 40-acre mining sites. The white frontiersmen had a favorite song in those days. Its opening lines were:

All I want in this creation
Is a pretty wife and a big plantation
Way down yonder in the Cherokee Nation.

As the Lottery winners forced their way onto their new property, Chief Ross and others were fighting the Removal Act with the powers in Washington. He pleaded with President Jackson for help. But no help came. However, there were many prominent whites who supported

the Cherokee cause and defended their rights. Noah Webster, John Adams, Sam Houston, and Davy Crockett were among the most famous defenders. President Jackson was not moved by their words or wisdom. Instead, he followed the demands of his friends who, in many cases, were primitive frontiersmen ready to seize Cherokee land. It is an ugly twist of fate that such ignorant men were considered better residents of the United States than the intelligent Cherokees.

The Cherokee leaders were not in complete agreement on how to deal with the Removal Act. After five years of unsuccessful legal efforts by Chief Ross, a small group took a fateful step. This group of 300 Cherokees, led by Major Ridge and his son John, signed the Treaty of New Echota with the U.S. government in 1835.

This treaty ceded to the United States all the Cherokee lands east of the Mississippi. In exchange, the Indians would receive rights in the Indian Territory (Oklahoma) plus 800,000 acres in what is now southeastern Kansas. The Indians were obliged to relocate within two years. The United States agreed to pay the cost of the migration plus living expenses for one year.

According to Cherokee law, Major Ridge and the other signers of this treaty acted illegally. Many were shocked by what Ridge did. He was considered a traitor. Years earlier he had executed another Cherokee who acted illegally by selling off Cherokee lands to whites. Now Ridge had done what he punished others for doing. Some suspected that Ridge had been bribed by U.S. officials. Shortly thereafter, both Ridges were assassinated by other Cherokees for participating in the Treaty of New Echota.

The United States Congress ratified the Treaty of New Echota by one vote. There were bitter arguments among the senators and representatives. Everyone knew that most Cherokees had not agreed to the treaty. In fact, more than 16,000 Cherokees petitioned the U.S. government to reject this treaty.

Chief Ross was defeated in his attempt to cancel this illegal document. In 1838, he would lead his people from the green Appalachian lands of their ancestors westward to the dry, often barren and unfamiliar Indian Territory.

The Removal Begins

The spring of 1838 arrived, and the time for the removal of the Cherokees to the West was to begin. But most Cherokees were not preparing for a journey. They ignored the orders of the Treaty of New Echota and continued to work in their fields. It appeared as if they believed the government would not follow through on the removal. But they believed falsely.

Soldiers of the U.S. Army invaded the territory daily. A total of 7,000 men under the direction of General Winfield Scott were ordered to carry out the removal. There was approximately one soldier for every two Indians.

General Scott hoped force would not be necessary. He distributed handbills throughout the Cherokee Nation asking the Indians to cooperate and move voluntarily. Only a few families did so. Scott then ordered his troops to scout the land, gathering and collecting all the Indians. He advised as little force as necessary. But a lot of force was used. Some soldiers and officers were rough and brutal, often striking their prisoners or poking them with their bayonets. Soldiers herded the Indians into groups like cattle. Children were separated from their families.

The removal of the Cherokees was a massive undertaking. Soldiers set up stockades as detention camps in several areas within the Cherokee lands. Each day squads would search a region and capture all the Indians they could find.

The Cherokees were taken from their fields with no opportunity to gather their belongings. Soldiers burst into Indian homes and dragged screaming families out. Women were forced to get up from their spinning wheels without a backward glance. Children were stopped in the middle of playing and dragged off to the stockade.

Usually the Cherokees left their homes with only the clothes on their backs. As they left, the new white owners were often ready to move into the cabin that sat on the land won in the Land Lottery.

Other whites followed the soldiers, so they could loot the abandoned cabins and houses. Fist fights and gun battles often occurred. Like vultures, these looting whites stuffed sacks with anything valuable that they could carry—clocks, silverware, musical instruments, jewelry.

The Indians were imprisoned in the camps until it was time to begin the journey west. By June nearly 3,000 Indians were assembled in the camps and forced to board boats that would carry them to their new homes in the Indian Territory west of the Mississippi River. The boat trip took them up to the Tennessee River to the Ohio, down the Mississippi, across the Arkansas River and into the land that one day would be called Oklahoma.

This trip was a painful journey. The summer heat made people sick. The small amount of food provided to them was often rotten. The boats were overcrowded and inadequate. But miraculously, most of the Indians survived to reach their new homeland.

The Trail of Tears

When Chief John Ross heard of the torturous river trip he asked General Scott to delay the departure of the remaining 12,000 Cherokees. It was agreed that they could wait until the fall when it would be cooler. And they would travel overland, not by water.

It was also agreed that Chief Ross could arrange with private contractors to transport his people. The Treaty of New Echota obligated the U.S. government to pay $65 for the migration expenses for each Indian—about eight cents a mile. With this money Ross contracted for 645 wagons and teams, plus tons of food. He hired guides and interpreters. Doctors were paid five dollars a day for their services along the route.

By October of 1838 the first group of 1,000 Cherokees started their long trek. Eleven more groups, each with 1,000 Indians, set out upon this cruel journey. The old and sick traveled in wagons, some rode horses, but most walked the entire distance of over 800 miles.

The trail went from Georgia northwest through Tennessee, into Kentucky, across the lower tip of Illinois, across Missouri and Arkansas. Traveling by land proved to be more torturous than the river journey. The Indians faced a bitterly cold winter ahead. The travelers suffered under freezing rain and snow. Most were poorly protected from the weather. At best, each had a blanket or two. The pain and agony of the travelers grieved Chief Ross. His grief was enlarged by the death of his own dear wife. Many lives could have been spared if the Indians had adequate supplies on the trip. But they did not. Many contractors were dishonest in their dealings with the Indians. The supplier delivered less than the agreed upon quantities in order to keep a hefty profit.

It was a time of misery. People wept and moaned as they moved. Wagons sunk in mud up to the axles, and exhausted Cherokees were expected to push and pull the wagons free. Many Indians got pneumonia and other serious illnesses. At each night's stop, the travelers would bury those who died that day. It was not unusual to bury fourteen bodies along the roadside.

At least 3,000 Cherokees died on this journey that the Indians called Nuna-da-ut-sun'y. In the Cherokee language that means, "the place where they cried." Later historians named this journey the "Trail of Tears." In 1988, 150 years after the event, President Ronald Reagan proclaimed the Trail of Tears a National Historic Trail. The memories of these tortured and heroic people would be at last honored by the government of the United States of America.

(Photo courtesy of Cherokee Indian Museum)

Tsali sacrificed his life for the good of his people.

The Story of Tsali

The removal of the eastern Cherokees did not mean the extermination of all Cherokees in the east. Today descendants of original Cherokees remain in North Carolina, thanks to the courage and sacrifice of a man named Tsali. His dramatic story is sad yet inspiring. It deserves retelling.

While U.S. soldiers were rounding up the Indians and imprisoning them in stockades, several hundred Cherokees escaped into the caves of the Great Smoky Mountains. One in that group was Tsali. As he struggled to avoid capture, he killed two soldiers. General Scott wanted Tsali found and punished for his crime, but the likelihood of finding Tsali was slim. Scott offered a painful compromise. He put out the word that all the Indians in hiding could have their freedom if Tsali turned himself in.

Tsali knew he would be executed if he left his hiding place. But he also knew he could enable his tribesmen to keep their homes in the lands of the ancestors. Tsali chose to sacrifice his life for others. According to legend, as Tsali faced the firing squad, his final words were, "It is sweet to die in one's own country."

These examples of Cherokee pottery have a distinctive "embossed" effect.

(Photos courtesy of Cherokee Indian Museum)

The Eastern Band

Today there are over 5,000 Cherokees living on the lands preserved for them by the sacrifice of Tsali. Known as the Eastern Band of Cherokee Indians, they reside on a reservation of more than 56,000 acres of land called Qualla Boundary. Its center is in Cherokee, North Carolina, but it is spread over five counties of the state.

Visitors can tour the Museum of the Cherokee Indians located there to view movies and exhibits documenting the history of the tribe. In the summer there is an outdoor performance called "Unto These Hills," which dramatizes the Cherokee story up to the Trail of Tears.

Cherokee life and customs of the 1700s are recreated in the Oconaluftee Village, which is a living museum. Visitors can walk among the Indians and talk with them as they demonstrate the Cherokee skills of basket weaving, pottery, cloth weaving, and other crafts.

Ancient Cherokee pottery had a distinctive style. The surface of a pot would have an impressed design. The simplest design might have been made by rolling or pressing an ear of corn over the pot while the clay was still wet. More complicated designs show circles within circles or interwoven lines. Archeologists found remains of pottery in the Southeast that were almost 4,000 years old.

Each Indian tribe can be identified by the early style and design of its baskets. Cherokee Indians used a simple method called plaiting—alternately crossing one strip over and under other strips. Often the weavers would cross the strips of material to form geometric patterns, such as diamond shapes. The rim of a Cherokee basket was also easy to identify. The Cherokees bent the ends of the woven material over a hoop to finish their baskets, while their neighbors, the Creeks, twisted the ends of materials into a braid.

Typical Cherokee baskets using white oak splints.

(Photo courtesy of Cherokee Indian Museum)

27

The Western Band

Following the forced migration to the Indian Territory, the Cherokee Nation immediately began to rebuild their culture in their new homeland. Life was very difficult in that land. Gone were the beautiful green hills and rich farmland. Gone, too, was the custom of individual ownership of land, a custom the Cherokees had copied from whites. Once again the Cherokees would own land in common as did their ancestors.

The Cherokees believed in the importance of education, and so by 1843 they had reestablished 18 schools. In 1851 they opened two colleges, called seminaries, one for men and one for women. Top scholars from these schools were sent to Princeton and other eastern universities.

As part of the Cherokee system of law enforcement, the Lighthorse Police were established. They were a group of mounted rangers who kept the Cherokee Nation free from the lawlessness that was common among white settlements in this age of the "Wild West."

One of the major jobs of the Lighthorse Police was dealing with whites who illegally sold liquor to the Indians. Since whites were actually foreigners in the Indian Territory, they could not be arrested for breaking Indian laws. All the Lighthorse could do with white intruders was to escort them to the border and warn them not to return.

When the Civil War between the Northern and Southern states began in 1861, the Cherokee Nation tried to remain neutral. But that was impossible. Cherokees were recruited by both the Northern army and the Confederate army of General Robert E. Lee. One Cherokee, Stand Watie, became a brigadier general in the Confederate army.

The Cherokee Nation was seriously divided by its views and support for that war. When the war ended, the Cherokees and all Indian tribes in the Territory were treated as a conquered enemy of the United States. The government forced

Cherokee boarding school.

A Cherokee girl holding her doll.

the building of railroads across the Indian Territory. In time this brought more white settlers to the region. These settlers eventually put demands on the federal government to make the area the state of Oklahoma.

When oil was discovered in the Indian Territory in 1904, the independence of the Indians living there was doomed. Like the discovery of gold in Georgia in 1828, this discovery meant wealth and power that the whites would not relinquish to the Indians. Three years later, the Indian Territory was declared the state of Oklahoma.

Although the Cherokees were unwilling to see their Nation become a part of the state, they were very important in shaping the new state. Several Cherokees were members of the Constitutional Convention. The first senator from Oklahoma was a Cherokee attorney, Robert Latham Owen, who served in Washington from 1907 to 1925.

It was not until 1924 that Indians of all tribes were granted citizenship in the United States. Up to that time and beyond, these Native Americans were

slowly becoming vanishing Americans. Many in all tribes suffered from poverty and lack of skills to maintain their self-support in the world of white industries. The United States government finally recognized its duty to help all Indians by passing the Indian Reorganization Act of 1934. That act provided federal money to help Indians develop new trades by which they could earn a living in the modern world.

Today there are more than 70,000 registered Cherokees across the country, and most reside in Oklahoma. In fact, the Cherokee tribe is the largest single Indian group in Oklahoma and the second largest in the United States. In Tahlequah, Oklahoma, visitors can tour the Tsaligi—meaning Cherokee—museum to view exhibits, movies, and a living recreated village that display the history of these proud, talented, and once powerful people. One need only look at the state seal of Oklahoma to see the position the Cherokee Nation of Oklahoma holds in the state. That seal bears a seven pointed star, which is also the symbol of the Cherokee Nation.

The seal of the Cherokee nation.

29

Important Dates in Cherokee History

1540s	Spanish explorer, Hernando DeSoto, travels Cherokee lands in search of gold.
1640s	French explorers begin trade with the Cherokees.
1754–1781	Cherokee warriors join forces with the British soldiers in the French and Indian Wars and the Revolutionary War.
1789–1791	Treaty of Tellico and Treaty of Holston—Cherokees lose most of their lands in North Carolina, South Carolina, and Tennessee.
1812–1814	Cherokee warriors join forces with Gen. Andrew Jackson in the War of 1812 and the Creek War.
1821	Sequoyah creates the syllabary of the Cherokee language—the first written Indian language.
1827	The constitution of the Cherokee Nation is written in Cherokee.
1828	A newspaper, the *Cherokee Phoenix,* is established.
1828	John Ross is elected Principal Chief of the Cherokee Nation.
1828	Gold is discovered on Cherokee land in Georgia.
1828	Andrew Jackson is elected President of the United States.
1830	U.S. Congress passes the Indian Removal Act that forces all Indians to move west of the Mississippi River.
1832	Georgia State Legislature passes Cherokee Land Lottery.
1835	Treaty of New Echota is signed between the U.S. government and an unauthorized group of Cherokees.
1838–1839	15,000 Cherokees make the forced migration to the Indian Territory. The journey is the "Trail of Tears."
1904	Oil is discovered in the Indian Territory (Oklahoma).
1907	Oklahoma becomes a state.
1924	U. S. government recognizes all Indians as citizens of the U.S.A.
1934	U.S. Congress passes Indian Reorganization Act that allows government to provide money for Indian development.
1988	President Ronald Reagan declares the "Trail of Tears" a National Historic Trail.

30

INDEX